# *Some Songs*

*Joseph Hart*

Science ............................................................. 39
Stranded ........................................................... 40
The Past ........................................................... 41
Gail ................................................................. 42
Lines ............................................................... 43
An Old Jingle ..................................................... 44
Maturity ........................................................... 45
Libido/Mortido ................................................... 46
The Lover .......................................................... 47
Love ................................................................ 48
Lines ............................................................... 49
Notre Dame ....................................................... 50
In New York ...................................................... 51
Friends ............................................................. 52
Beauty .............................................................. 53
The Doll ........................................................... 55
The Beetle ......................................................... 56
The Bee ............................................................ 57
Love ................................................................ 58
When Maxx Got In Bed With Me ............................... 59
A Saying ........................................................... 60
A Moment .......................................................... 61
Lines ............................................................... 62
Keats ............................................................... 63
Dickinson .......................................................... 64
Archaeology ....................................................... 65
Which? ............................................................. 66
The Battle .......................................................... 67
Maya ............................................................... 68
Chauvet ............................................................ 69
A Metaphor ........................................................ 70
Maxx Asleep ....................................................... 71
The Gift ............................................................ 72
Love ................................................................ 73
Fred ................................................................ 74
The Dying Poet .................................................... 75
Time ................................................................ 76

Death .......................................................................................... 77
The Rose .................................................................................... 78
Futility ...................................................................................... 79
Back From Oz ........................................................................... 80
Perfect Poems ........................................................................... 81
In The Subway .......................................................................... 82
Joyce's Poems ........................................................................... 83
Emily Bronte ............................................................................. 84
Lost ........................................................................................... 85
Cats ........................................................................................... 86
Men ........................................................................................... 87
Questions ................................................................................... 88
E.L. ........................................................................................... 89
A Coward's Song ...................................................................... 90
The Deist ................................................................................... 91
Reading "The Rubaiyat" ............................................................ 92
J.S. ............................................................................................. 93
"To Helen" ................................................................................ 94
Poets ......................................................................................... 95
Lines .......................................................................................... 96
Lines .......................................................................................... 97
Peace ......................................................................................... 98
A Single Book ........................................................................... 99
Maxx ....................................................................................... 100
Lines ........................................................................................ 101
On Killing ................................................................................ 102
Music ....................................................................................... 103
Freddy ..................................................................................... 104
Modern Art .............................................................................. 105
Freddy ..................................................................................... 106
A Tragedy ................................................................................ 107
Four Limericks ........................................................................ 108
Lines ........................................................................................ 109
Fred ......................................................................................... 110
Animals ................................................................................... 111
A Prayer .................................................................................. 112
JKD, another love song .......................................................... 113

# By The Sea

Living alone
Beside the sea -
Only music,
A cat and me -


Forgetting what never
Could have been -
Watching the waves
Go out, come in -


A gull in a mist
Upon a post
Is lost in the fog -
A feathered ghost -

# On The Mental Ward

On the mental ward
Staring at the wall -
Or he paced corridor –
That's what he did - that's all.


A preacher came to ease
His madness and his doubt.
He talked about salvation.
That's what preachers talk about.

The mental patient answered
In a whisper, not a shout -
"It's very pretty nonsense;
But it's nonsense.
Please get out."

# The Cat

I'm standing in the midnight
Begging God to save
My body from the madhouse
Or the final grave


While my cat's alive -
All living things are cursed!
Wishing that my cat
Gets to heaven first.

# Lines

I am like a man
Who sits alone and drinks
And says that what he thinks
Isn't what he thinks.


In a world of chance
I'm sure – I don't know how -
Nothing bad can happen;
My book is published now.

# Maxx

The cat sleeps by my face
With my arm around him.
Neither of us stirs,
Together in the darkness.
And it makes me happy
When he purrs.

# A Jingle

I never believe a thing
In the sky or the terrain
Lest I believe the madness
And go totally insane.

# Love

I believe that love
Is the same in all the species -
A gentle similarity -
But the thread is broken.

# God

If by chance there were a God -
A gentle God and kind -
In a world that makes no sense -
And possibly a heaven -


But many many animals
And people on the earth
Since it all began -


"Since it all began" -
When was that?
And how was that?
And all without a God -

# MAGA

"Make America Great Again" -
Backward we shall go
To the days of Joe McCarthy,
The evil of Jim Crow,
Keeping gays in closets,
And women's status low -

# The Accident

Driving down the road one night
Suddenly there was
Someone in my headlights.
Did I hit him?
I swerved and hit a post.
Some people said to go.
He wasn't there; I looked.
Before I drove away,
A person on the street
Got into my car,
Frightened me and took
My cell and went away.
At home I called a cop
Who took down a report.
I later called the station and
They sent me the report.
It only said
My cell phone had been stolen.

# Lines

So many many people
Looking at the sky -
Nothing there but stars -
Pretending they know why.


How beautiful the dream!
Relinquished – sadly I
Just hope to see my cats
In heaven ere I die.


Then a final paradox -
Ridiculous is prayer! -
The Jesus of my youth -
I still believe he's there.


Gentle, gentle Jesus -
As though he knows me well -
Who's saving me with love.
Religion is a spell.


A very sweet illusion -
That is all I've got.
Very very clearly,
He is not.

# Evil

Evil is! Evil is!
Unrepentant horrors -
Denizens of hell
Free on the earth.


They make the common crimes
Of ordinary people
Nothing – needing only
Very slight forgiveness.


What is in the mind
Of an evil man -
A sadist now – who once
Was a little child?

# Lines

The poetry I write
Is not the poetry they read.
It's published now.
The people I have known -
Every one of them
Is either old or dead.
Success – a hollow happiness
Alone.

# Keats' Poems

Walking through a garden
On a winter day -
Pictures and sensations -
Where I want to stay.


A melody that's sweet -
No "cloying melody" -
Embracing all my senses -
Where I want to be.

# Treasures

The treasures in my room -
Horowitz and Proust -
Pictures on the walls -
Curios on shelves -


Connected to the world -
Unable to break free -
Are everything to me -
And indifferent to you -

# Ideas

When I felt the ribs
Of the cat I thought,
"This can't be Evolution".
A heartless God?  Or what?


The universe has edges.
That is what she said.
It's difficult to think;
But what is true instead?

# The Animals

I'm completely unselfconscious
When I'm with my cat.
Are animals uncritical?
Yes!  I'll tell you that.


Aging and forgotten,
I have ceased to rove.
Finally I've found
Something I can love.


Do people love the animals?
They love themselves instead.
When they meet an animal,
The people shoot him dead.


People do not care
When the harmless grieve.
People care for nothing,
Except what they believe.

# The Modern Poet

He'll tell you it is meaningful,
He'll tell you it is new,
And better than an atavistic ditty.
But what a modern poet
Can never say to you
Is that it is poetical or pretty.

# My Cat & Burns

The depth of grief and sadness,
Understanding in your eyes.
Despite the thought of Burns, Cat,
What do you know of death?


You sat.  I stood there stroking
Your forehead down your back,
And saw such lonely wisdom
As you stared up at me,
Sadness and such wisdom
As you looked up at me.

8-12-13

# Horowitz, Horszowski

Horowitz, Horszowski -
I listen to them play
While looking at their pictures.
Old but beautiful were they.


Music lasts forever.
Just musicians die.
There's something in the earth,
If there is nothing in the sky.

# Cats

The happiness of ownership!
I'm looking at a cat
With a roll of colored yarn.
It's his.
Do cats do what they do
Everywhere, forever?

# Music

Ashkenazy, Horowitz,
Brendel, Cziffra, Schiff,
Perahia - are the planets
Circling in my night -
Planets that reflect the light
Of Mozart, Haydn, Bach.

# Maxx

When the little kitten
Sticks his nose into my nostril,
Bites my ear
Or sleeps against my chest,
I think there is a God
Or maybe love
Of maybe something.
But what's the use?
We're aging anyway.

# A Martian Poem

Cats are fond of love,
I think, and what is more,
When they're allowed to live,
They know the score.

# The Doctor

He asked the wise psychologist,
"Do I love my cat?
I react as if I do.  But doctor,
I don't feel a thing.
Am I deeply phony?
Am I possibly insane?"
The doctor smiled profoundly and said,
"No.  You're just an ass."

# Begun Happy

Captured like a butterfly on cork -
I never meant for verse to set me free  -
My rainy little sojourn in New York
Was for writing shows, not poetry.


Why do I write songs?  I simply do it.
In a script like actors in a play.
If there's a reason, then I never knew it.
Cadavers in a coffin have to stay.


To live in constant hate and not to die -
Under water in a fetid bay -
The vixen's not intelligent, it's sly -
Don't exist.  You'll get in someone's way.

# Prosody

Once when I was young -
I was once, was I not? -
Poetry and lyrics
Were my chosen lot.
What is verse?  I wondered.
I thought and thought and thought
About it, and it seemed
It's rhythm, rhyme - and what?

# Keats

Like a silver star,
Junkets' verses sing,
Hanging in the cosmos,
Not attached to anything.


Neither are they personal
And neither history,
But cold and unapproachable
Perfect poetry.

# Lines

Callas said music was
Meant to be soothing.
Keats wrote a beautiful poem.
Neither one matches the art or the world
Of today, but I cling to them,
Thrashing, a drowning man
Holding a log at sea.

# Live Things

Live things kill each other,
Not only just to eat.
Children needing love
Are sleeping in the street.


For the soul to keep
The personality alive,
People are rejected,
And only just survive.


Animals become
The property of Man.
Can it be avoided?
I don't see how it can.


Just a cruel God
Could look down and love it.
Ineffectual!
Make poems of it!

# Values

After the ball is over
And they call out, "Change partners again!"
Do you sashay back to the first one,
And think of what might have been?


Are you old fashioned and dreamy
Believing in Jesus, not luck,
Problems with only one answer,
And happiness more than a fuck?


That middle class love is what matters,
That madness and aging are lies,
Everyone's basically decent,
And only a person cries?

# Lines

Standing in the gutter,
I'm barking at the world!
Damn it! I believe my songs are good!
I've written many poems
And bound them into books,
More poems than I ever thought I would.


All my life is messy.
None of it makes sense.
I can't say, "I did this and therefore that."
Poems grew like flowers
In a pile of shit,
Where also grow the nettles and the weeds.

# Science

Science is experiment,
Reason, observation.
Who the hell can be opposed to this?
Poke out both your eyes,
Work up a sensation,
And never think:
Religion gives you bliss.

# Stranded

Evolution seems
So silly it's absurd -
The whiskers on a cat -
All the feathers on a bird.


And creationism's bogged
In such an awful mire
Of moral Christian fictions,
Bigotry and fire.


That leaves me where I'm standing
With nowhere left to go.
There's nothing to believe
And even less to know.

# The Past

I'm living in a past I know is gone.
Memories like ghosts
Not contained by cemeteries
Linger in my consciousness like dreams.


Like an aging woman
Jilted in her youth,
Wearing still the veil she wore before,
I'm sitting in the lace
Fallen to decay,
And looking at some phantoms that don't age.

# Gail

You said you liked my poems.
You said it many times -
The clumsy, awkward rhythms
And stale rhymes.


I'm sure you are in heaven.
You left behind a need -
I've written better poems
That you will never read.

# Lines

Some people have a lover
With the happiness it brings.
Years ago, the artists
Made poetry that sings.
Americans would scorn
To change their state with kings.
Mine's a sweet content
And happiness with things.

# An Old Jingle

Elizabeth, Lizzie, Betsy and Bess
All went to town in the very same dress.
One said  "no," one said "yes,"
One said "maybe" and one said "guess!"
Elizabeth, Lizzie, Betsy and Bess,
Standing there wearing the very same dress
All of a sudden began to regress,
Which bothered the neighbors, more or less.

# Maturity

I know that cops are mean.
I know that shrinks are mad.
And preachers have the smallest minds
A person ever had.


But after I come in
From the cold, dark, cynic night,
Relax and pet my cat
In happiness and light,
Regardless of tomorrow's
Confusion and chagrin,
Like a simple child
I trust them all again.

# Libido/Mortido

It takes a man of genius -
Infinitely rare -
To make a thing of beauty
With conscionable care.


It only takes a vulgar man -
With bigotries to spare -
Maybe half a minute
To blow it into air.


Then it isn't there.

# The Lover

Is love a fool?
Love that has compassion.
Compassion for a stranger.  Strangers come
With appetites and knives.  It's not a fool
If it wounded then desists to love,
And runs to those who care.
But love does not.
Love's a fool,
A martyr with no God.

# Love

Love's an ugly thing.
It makes paupers out of men,
Uses up their youth
So they can never love again.


Insidious and cold,
It's a hateful game to play.
As the killer leaves,
The dying whispers, "Stay!"

# Lines

Kitty, Jay and Gary
Haunt this poetry,
Coming through the guilt
Like spectres from the sea.
I was worse to them
Than anyone to me.

# Notre Dame

Notre  Dame's
Gone up in flames
And the old American liar
Belches twice
And tweets advice
To the people fighting the fire.

# In New York

I was in New York.
I went out one night
To a curbside market
Somewhere on the street.


I meant to buy a sandwich
When a man behind me
Asked me for my change
After I was done.


I told him I had only
Enough.
There'd be no change.


However, there was change
And he followed me
Shouting – I was frightened -
That I was a liar.

# Friends

If you make a friend
Whose interests are yours -
Same music, books and movies,
Same pictures – hold him close.
He's rare, he's very rare.
Such love is gold.


But if your love is rap,
Stephen King and rock,
Homicide in movies
Sex without surcease,
You needn't be so fussy.
Such interests are legion.
You'll always have a friend.
You'll never be alone.

# Beauty

My aim.  To follow Keats.
An odyssey of love!
A poet who loved beauty
And had no point to prove.


Are poets after beauty?
Starting with the Greeks
It was the final end
That every artist seeks.


They're yelling in the temple.
Beauty?  They eschew it.
They holler, "I'm an artist!"
But none of them can do it.


"Beauty". I can't say it.
Like a dying flame,
Something that's poetical
Was my only aim.


I call their poems bad.
This is much too bold.
I recognize the dross.
Can mine be gold?

This is what I think.
Shall I tell it to
Winners of awards
Who will not think it's true?


Beauty is a phantom,
A frigate on the sea.
Beauty is illusion.
What is poetry?

# The Doll

I'm a bumptious little boy
Playing with a cotton doll,
Mine alone.  I own this toy,
More sweetly than a truck or ball.


Keats.  I'm never long without
My ragged doll, inanimate,
A thing I rip and toss about
As I like.  We share a fate.


I need no phantom cherubim.
Every night he sleeps with me.
I've torn a dozen holes in him,
Scorned and loved his poetry.

# The Beetle

As hopeless as a hobo,
An itinerant who begs,
A helpless beetle on its back
Was lying, and its legs

Were thrashing.  It was dying
On the pavement.  That was plain.
And every tiny jerk was an
Expression of its pain.

"God is evil!" I was thinking.
"Let your Deity be hung!
Harmless while alive this creature
Only wanted dung!"

As I stood and watched to my
Relief it's sweet to say,
It flipped onto its stomach
And simply crawled away.

# The Bee

A bee with a broken wing
Is lying on the ground.
A hundred ants converge on it and bite.
Its other wing is beating.
It doesn't make a sound,
Except its buzz grows fainter.  Now no flight


Is possible.  It's dying.
Once autonomous and gold,
It wasn't born alone.  Alone it cries.
The ants without compassion,
Mechanical and cold,
Kill it.  In the end it only dies.

# Love

Stale beer and cheap motel rooms -
Winds that whistle silently
Through old ruins -


Breathless ghosts of people, thoughts
And feelings – love
That never was – is it
All illusion,
Guesses, hope
And fantasy?


Passing music that in age
Will be as common, unremembered
As the prehistoric night -

# When Maxx Got In Bed With Me

Mammals need affection.
The heart is in the brain.
Flowers only need
Manure, dirt and rain.
Surrender your autonomy,
And you will go insane.

# A Saying

Walking through the woods without a compass -
Looking at Picasso when you're blind -
Seeking without any hope of finding
Someone who is reasonable and kind -

# A Moment

A prisoner in a cell or on hard labor,
Dead to all, not numb, but just enduring -
Enduring but to what?  There is no end. -
Feels a kind of love or brief affection
When the warder says a gentle thing,
But then goes back to brutalizing him.

# Lines

"God is love," the prophets said.
In spite of death and pain.
All life responds to love.  Instead
The people go insane.


But animals will only live,
And Man is not above
Kittens who, although they give,
Don't make a God of love.

# Keats

Keats abjured ideas -
His injunction: Do not think.
In spite of my devotion,
I do nothing else.


Keats is very pretty.
His poetry like music
Seduces all the senses,
And delights a child.


What have I to offer?
When the castle falls,
All the thoughts will crumble;
Flowers will remain.

# Dickinson

Her melodies on God,
Clover bells and bees,
Heaven and eternity and birds -
All her tiny poems
On subjects such as these
Are precious – too much so
For clumsy words.

# Archaeology

Biblical names and arrow heads,
Pottery and jars,
Oceans and volcanoes,
Golden tombs and wars!


What became of the poetry?
Scarabs, pharaohs, rings!
What became of the music?
Gods and graves and kings!

# Which?

Keats or Shostakovich?
Which is it to be?
Self or selfless magic
In poetry?


Keats said in a song
The self must not appear.
In such a situation
Is anything sincere?


But Shostakovich said
Put personality
And nothing else in music.
Is this poetry?

# The Battle

Firing from the battlements
While all the soldiers slept,
Shooting at innumerable
Enemies that kept


Coming, just like roaches
Everywhere he stepped -
Finally he threw aside
His pistol and just wept.

# Maya

Archaeology – stories of war,
Sacrifices and tombs replete
With gold and jade and
The servants of kings
And pathways into heavens.

# Chauvet

A million million years ago, The Artist.
He painted, but he did not paint himself.
He drew like Keats and Wilde from empathy.
A thousand pictures covering the walls!
Men like him discovering today
The pictures in the silence of a cave,
No gods perhaps, but deities unformed,
Mammoths, deer and horses – on the walls,
Art as an example of the soul,
Forgotten now, but genius will create.
The immortality of Art itself!

# A Metaphor

Today I understand
What I didn't know.
I don't make decisions.
I'm an ocean wave,
Superficial, shallow,
That slips across the sand,
Circling but not stopping
At any certain stone.

# Maxx Asleep

Watching Maxx asleep -
His whiskers twitch,
He licks his lips,
And a quiver in his paw,
A little jerk -
While he is sleeping -


He partly opes his eyes.
I say his name.
He doesn't hear me.
His eyes go slowly closed again,
And he continues sleeping.

# The Gift

He bought a little pistol
That popped a bit of paper.
It was just a toy.
We were very young.


His family was poor.
The pistol was a present.
That night we slept together
In a giant bed.


And I tried to touch him.
He looked at me with hatred.
He had offered love.
I wanted sex.

# Love

Don't let Vesuvius erupt on us, Maxx,
A cat but not a pet,
More precious to me than anyone
I have ever met,
Except two boys when I was a boy
Whom I shall not forget
Until I die and the world is gone.
It hasn't happened yet.

# Fred

Cats are very sensual,
But what they like is love.
When they touch your nose it isn't
Sex, it is affection.


But if they die abandoned
On a sidewalk or a road,
They're gone, and love goes with them.
Life – provisional and precious.

# The Dying Poet

The poet lay in bed
Dying, and he thanked
God who'd let him live until
He'd written one last poem.
While children slept in cages
And their fathers killed themselves.
The devil smiled.
He had another soul.

# Time

Thousands of years of poetry
That someone thought divine
Are gone.  Here in the evening,
I am writing mine.


Tomorrow is forever.
Yesterday for years -
Archaeology remembers,
Until it disappears.

# Death

For thousands and thousands and thousands of years
Nothing ever changes.
Temples are built, and cats who love
Are sacrificed for kings.


Peat collects upon a fen.
A glacier covers corpses.
Tombs are built for special people
By forgotten men.


Nonjudgmental children love
Whatever mothers hold them,
Grow up and love the fatherland
As patriotic bigots.

# The Rose

The saddest scene I ever saw -
Shocking and abhorrent -
A photo of a rose -
Faster than it actually occurred -
An image of a bud -
Then in a couple seconds,
It opened and it spread into a bloom -
Several seconds more,
It withered and turned brown,
And finally hung wilted on the stem.

# Futility

I keep writing poems
In an artless age.
I often wonder what I do it for.
I've read modern verse -
Neither beautiful nor sage -
Which even if it rhymed would be a bore.

# Back From Oz

"The Wizard of Oz" is a lot of fun,
But I must appeal
To sense.  Perhaps she dreamed the witch,
But old Miss Gulch is real,
And she'll be back for the dog when Dorothy's
Head begins to heal.

# Perfect Poems

Crimson flowers, pretty concepts,
Oceans curling on the shore,
Trees that stoop and touch the grass,
Skies of sunlight, skies of rain -


These are poems.  Does a poet
Try to write them anymore?
Who said form is beauty?  And
Will even beauty last ?

# In The Subway

He was standing on the edge
Of the concrete platform
In the subway tunnel -
And he didn't fall.


A woman said he had
A lovely sense of balance.
There were no trains passing -
And he didn't fall.


I thought he looked embarrassed.
Carefully he balanced,
His arms reached out beside him -
And he didn't fall.

# Joyce's Poems

The most beautiful poems I ever read -
Delicate and fey,
Fanciful and limpid -
Like a shell found by the sea -
Thin, translucent, grey.

# Emily Bronte

Is Bronte less substantial than Keats?
The nothingness of feelings
That passes.  When it's gone
It is forgotten.


But at the time seems solid - like a swell
That hits the shore and bursts
Into countless waves
Of water and froth that
In the air disperse.


Poetry I feel and want to touch -
Like holding ghosts -
For a moment beautiful
And mine -
Though never mine.

# Lost

"Treat me like I matter."
That is what he said.
He gave them all he had.
They took it.  And instead
Of giving him affection,
They hit him in the head,
And left him in the road,
Thinking he was dead.

# Cats

When a cat is sad, you will not know it.
He will suffer, but he will not grieve.
That's how nature made him.  God knows why.


When a cat is sick, he will not show it.
Stoical and precious, he will leave
The things that made him happy, and just die.

# Men

Horrible people, despicable names -
Death behind a smile -
Out of the slime – like kittens and dogs -
What makes men so vile?


Kittens and dogs, mice and slugs
Have nothing when life is done.
The lovers of Hitler and Donald Trump
Are Christians, every one.


Is this what the clamor of ugly voices
Have yelled vociferously -
That Rand and the Bible can justify
Any atrocity?

# Questions

Does Jesus love a fly
Or the feelings of a cat?
Do people who are crazy
Or ugly go to God?


So many small details
Lost to your devotion,
Sloughed aside and silenced
By the guns of your belief.

# E.L.

When I was young, he said to me,
"Read, read philosophy,"
Then let the other slipper fall:
"When you're done, forget it all."


A mind like his – above the herd -
To whom the world must seem absurd.
Yesterday I saw him: old,
A mindless, smiling ember – cold.

# A Coward's Song

Cats don't have the pride
And dignity of men.
When they are afraid, they turn and run.
People aren't like this.
They bravely stand, and then
They're honored by their fathers,
And lie buried in the sun.

# The Deist

Something made the universe -
I don't know what it was
Or whether there was anything at all.
I assume it was a presence
I'll call a deity.
It never was a kindly one,
Compassionate or fair;
If there's even anything,
Anybody there.

# Reading "The Rubaiyat"

Like looking in the dark until
A dozen stars appear,
I read these poems over until
What they say is clear.

# J.S.

They fell like flies
Beneath her spell,
Or Eurydice in hell.


On a gibbet
Each one hung
From her autocratic tongue.


Her self-esteem
Knocked giants down;
Hers the only game in town.


Drawn like magic
To her name;
Moths attracted to a flame.


A few stood up
And walked away,
Not hypnotized,
And would not play.

# "To Helen"

### (inspired by a misreading of a poem by Hesse)

Hopelessness has scarred her.
She gently lies abed.
Potential lovers pass her
Thinking she is dead.


The moon is shining on her.
Stars are bits of coal.
Forever night is hiding
The scars upon her soul.


Can she hear a nightingale,
Or the ocean break?
Will there be a morrow?
Will the night awake?

# Poets

I don't know how he did it.
When genius gripped his soul,
What he wrote was magic.
Diamonds from coal!


Robinson, Millay
Wrote warm and gentle things;
But Junkets' poetry
Beautifully sings.


Other folks find other
Poets more divine
Than the several poets
I consider mine.


Like I find my cat,
My very precious Maxx.
Shall I forget the world,
And with what I love relax?

# Lines

In a long, black coat,
And it was filthy on the back,
In dirty yellow stockings,
No shoes, and tangled hair,


She came into the taco store;
And while I sat there watching,
She ordered;
And I thought she must have money.


A couple other women, young,
Came in and stood and waited.
The indigent was fumbling,
But I couldn't hear her.


Then one of the young women,
Without flourishes or fuss,
Crisply said, "I'll pay!"
And she was Jesus.

# Lines

The poetry I used to write
Wasn't good because
Of what I did,
But rather what I was.


Shall I weigh my anchor
And leave this peaceful sea
Of Keats, and sail uncharted
Into modern poetry?

# Peace

Maxx slept in my lap
For over half an hour.
While he did, a mood came over me.
I didn't know in nature
There was such a power
That heals –
But music or good poetry.

# A Single Book

To write a signal novel
Like "The Stranger" by Camus
Or "Jean Santeuil" - a single book
Significant alone,
Something that a little boy
Can cherish as his own.

# Maxx

I don't know if I love you.
Does it matter, little bear?
I like you by my chest
Sleeping there.


And when you do not come -
As for a spell you don't -
I die.
But will I die?  I won't.

# Lines

At home in her madness,
An egg in its shell,
Neither touching nor touched,
As if under a spell,


When will her words
Like the face on a doll
Or like water through fingers,
Mean nothing at all?


Writing a poem
Or smiling obliquely,
Hopelessly hoping,
And living too meekly,


Faces and masks
She tacked to her wall,
She trusts but untrusting,
Expecting to fall.


Living in silence,
Too often opposed;
Preachers are bastards,
The church's door closed.

# On Killing

People kill and they always did -
In every soul a hun -
For food, for Gods, for bigotry,
For fun.

# Music

Music makes you fall in love.
Music make you go to war.
Music makes you feel there is
A God and you're divine.
Music helps you drink your beer.
Music lowers your defenses.
Music makes you burst with tears
Of camaraderie.

9-30-12

# Freddy

To lie upon my lap and curl your feet up,
A length of string to leap into the air with,
Another unsuspecting cat to beat up,
Two intent green eyes to stand and stare with -
The world allowed you these to make you glad -
And it gave you to me when I am sad.

11-11-12

# Modern Art

Look at Bernini and hide your face.
Hear Wilde and cease to talk.
Read Keats and Millay and keep your place.
And blush when you hear Bach.

# Freddy

A creature as loving and gentle as this
Should never die, should never die.
But he will, I tell you;
Though I don't know why, I don't know why.

# A Tragedy

The farmer left his house
With a mallet and a gun.
"I'm going to kill that dog," he thought,
"And it will be fun."


The little boy just watched.
It was an easy kill.
He didn't do a thing.
And God was very still.


The days continued on,
Though nothing lay ahead.
"I let him kill my dog,"
Was all he ever said.

# Four Limericks

There once was a fellow named Jack
Who gave it a wonderful whack
Which wasn't as odd
As the length of his rod
Which allowed him to whack from the back.


A feisty old fellow with cheek
And joints so archaic they creak
Kept getting crushes
On girls with small tushes
And sneaking about for a peek.


A man who was terribly kind
Had a penis he had to unwind.
It bent in the middle.
He cried, "I can't piddle
Because I'm so badly designed!"


Exceeding my place and my station,
I leap to my feet in elation.
This limerick's dirt,
But I'll give you my shirt
If it isn't my greatest creation!

# Lines

I just watched a cop
Dancing in the street
With a little Black kid.
Watching it was sweet.
Affection is a thing
Hate cannot defeat.

# Fred

I wish that all the cats in the world
Were petted, just like Fred -
Not alone in a wilderness,
Unwanted and unfed,
To run alone, afraid and cold,
Til finally they're dead.

# Animals

Small bodies –
But not a small mind -
Look at an animal -
That's what you'll find.


A cat will love you
If you let him,
And spread his ears
So you can pet him.

# A Prayer

God, don't let me die before my cats do.
A gift for them -
A final  gift for me.
Though the horrors of your world,
Both past and present,
Refute a tender-hearted deity.

# JKD, another love song

Jay in Jersey.  Not
The only friend I've had.
But one that I remember.
Not a thing was sad.


I met him in the library
In a quiet nook
Listening to love songs
While I read a book.


Totally uncritical,
Or else he did not see
Anything to criticize.
In happy irony,


He laughed, "You are a poet!"
What became of Jay?
He went back to India.
I just went away.


A winter passed in Hackensack,
Provincial little town.
He'd holler, "Fucking Hackensack!"
As the snow came down.

He was dark and pretty,
With hair as black as night.
I was only happy.
Everything was right.


Every day we'd visit
As evening drew near.
I would drink a soda.
He would drink a beer.


He said to get the forms
At the embassy
One needs to move to India.
I figured he meant me.


I pretended not to know
Why he wanted them.  And he
In a rush of anger,
Threw them back at me.


He left me standing there -
Foolish in the rain.
He left.  I left.  And we
Never met again.


I've always had the fantasy
I saw him one time more -
Listening to records
As he'd done before.

www.ingramcontent.com/pod-product-compliance
Lightning Source LLC
LaVergne TN
LVHW090157180726
843489LV00006B/2098